Get Rich ASF

The Transformative Money Mindset for Life-Changing Success

by

Tanya J. Brown

Table of contents

Introduction

Money plays an important role in our lives. It gives us the means to care for our fundamental needs, follow our passions, and accomplish our objectives. But many people frequently need clarification on whether they earn enough money to be financially stable and live comfortably. You must establish your financial objectives before determining whether you are earning enough money. Consider your short- and long-term goals, like debt repayment, retirement savings, home ownership, or business startup. You can calculate the income necessary to support your aspirations by setting clear goals.

Examine your income honestly and contrast it with your goals and financial responsibilities. Compute your monthly expenditures, encompassing bills, housing/lease, groceries, travel, and extravagance purchases. Assess the amount you are saving and whether it corresponds with your objectives. This assessment will shed light on your financial circumstances.

Your earning potential can be considerably impacted by consistently investing in your education and skill set. Determine what needs to be improved in your field and look for advanced degrees, certifications, or courses that will address those needs. More experience boosts your employability and leads to better-paying jobs or business ventures.

Making more money is only one aspect of maximizing your earning potential; another is prudent money management. Make a budget, keep tabs on your spending, and give investing and saving top priority.

Chapter 1

Knowing How to Make Money

There needs to be a curriculum in personal finance at school. It implies that having financial difficulties as an adult is quite common. Being unable to handle your finances well may be the biggest obstacle to your professional advancement.

Your income is likely a salary if you are moving up the corporate ladder. If you're further along in life, you likely have some investments and are planning for emergencies or retirement.
However, let's assume that your corporate salary is your only source of income. And how do you optimize your earnings?

The sum of income minus expenses equals earnings. This is a straightforward mathematical calculation; it's not rocket science. When you're willing to learn more about debt, interest, return on investment, and other financial concepts you'll need to comprehend throughout your life, things can get complicated.

Five Ways to Increase Your Income:

1: Discuss a pay raise. Request a pay increase. Even though it should be apparent, only some people ask for raises based on the value they bring to their employers rather than their own needs. Learn the strategy that your employer is using. Aim for the same flow, produce measurable work, and add value to it. Beginning your request for a pay increase by stating that you require additional funds to meet your mortgage, debts, or other personal obligations is the worst course of action.

2. Establish precise pay goals for the following five years. Create your pay ladder by considering your current income and your desired 5-year career path. There are a few intermediate steps. Regardless of the organization you work for, have the roles and responsibilities you are creating for yourself. It will be simpler for you to decide when to change jobs or apply for a promotion if you clearly understand your goal.

3. Excel in your field to the fullest. Develop your ability to assign and implement procedures. One option is to give work to an individual, but this is the most costly approach from a business standpoint.

Alternatively, you can create processes and assign work to teams and automated tools. Your productivity will increase due to those actions, and you'll have more time for operational tasks. Recall that job overload and overtime are the biggest obstacles to maximizing your pay. It would help if you immediately let go of the notion that you are the only one who can do this and that you should be doing it all. Nobody is.

4. Invest in yourself. The best way to stay employable is to always continue learning. To survive, you must acquire new abilities and gain more knowledge on subjects you are interested in. This dispels the notion that a college degree is sufficient to launch a successful career and creates a plan for lifelong learning.

5. Make use of your contacts in the business world. Using your network to find new employment is best if you realize your current position could be more suitable for you in the long run. Choose those who are willing to support your growth and who are acquainted with you.

For many job seekers, pay is a crucial consideration, and there are numerous ways to increase your income to better support your needs. Many people wish to enhance their income for various reasons, including debt repayment, future savings, emergency funding, and comfortable living. Even though many variables can influence your pay, knowing some tactics you can use to boost your earning potential may help you achieve your objectives.

Advantages of raising your income
Increasing your income has several benefits, such as:

1. Stress reduction: Raising your income may ease any concerns about your financial management skills.
2. Increasing your income could help stabilize your earnings because some people's pay is based on sales and hours worked.
3. Assisting you in reaching your objectives: Having more income may make it simpler for you to start a retirement account, save money for future purchases, or pay off debt.

Consider whether you want to increase your pay in the short or long term when creating a plan to increase your income. This might aid you in selecting the best strategy to accomplish your objective. For instance, you might use a short-term solution if you want to make extra money to pay for a planned trip. A long-term fix, like a raise, might work better if your goal is to raise your take-home income permanently. Considering any additional tax obligations brought on by increased income is crucial.

Ten methods to boost your income

You could use a range of tactics to increase your income. Remember that your pay may vary depending on your experience, location, and employer; some strategies may work better than others. When trying to increase your income, try to set reasonable expectations. Here are 10 strategies you could try to improve your chances of earning more money:

1.   Return to school.

Acquiring an advanced degree could open up new career options if you're interested in aiming for a more prestigious title and a higher salary. Look into career advancement opportunities in your field to see if you need a degree to accomplish your objectives. Graduate degrees, such as master's or doctorate degrees, can expand your network and help you gain more profound industry knowledge, which could position you for greater responsibility at work. If you aim to use your experience to enter a different field, you might also get ready to change careers.

Some employers encourage their staff members to pursue postsecondary education to boost their work abilities and productivity. Many employers even reimburse all or a portion of an employee's tuition costs if they pursue an advanced degree. To find out if you can receive tuition reimbursement to assist with paying for your education, think about conversing with an HR representative at your place of employment.

2. Establish a source of passive income

You can boost your income without going through training or college by generating passive income. Any form of payment that requires little to no active labour is considered passive income. Investing in rental properties, offering ads on social media, or selling downloadable assets online are ways to generate passive income. Even though these pursuits may initially take a lot of time and work, they can complement your income from your job without requiring a break.

3. Examine the benefits you now offer to employees. Many companies provide employee benefits that allow workers to save money. A few examples of these perks include a flexible spending account (FSA), 401(k) options, and travel reimbursements for parking, gas, or public transportation. Additionally, some employers provide programs for childcare assistance and tuition reimbursement. With these benefits, you can save money for retirement, pay for health care, and live more affordably. Arranging a meeting with an HR representative could prove advantageous in gaining additional knowledge about the benefits at your disposal.

4. Adjust your withholdings on taxes

You can quickly increase your take-home pay by modifying the amount of tax deducted from your paycheck. As soon as the following pay period arrives, this gives you a larger paycheck. Remember that at the end of the year, you are still responsible for paying taxes on your income. Consult a financial advisor or an HR representative at work to comprehend your options and choose the best option within your means.

5. Launch a side venture

Launching a side business is another innovative way to earn extra money. There are several approaches to this, many of which require minimal time and financial commitment. You could perform your hobbies for others for pay if they interest the general public. For instance, you may use your excellent camera to take client portraits professionally or use your weekends to offer freelancing writing services. Consider taking up babysitting or pet sitting as a side gig.

6. Earn a certification

Professional certifications help you grow your skills, qualify for new positions, and prove your value to your employer. You can use several resources to take a program and achieve certification, and many of these programs can be completed online anytime. Research the certifications available in your career and consider getting one to grow your career. Remember that certification could strengthen your resume and connect you to new opportunities, but only some employers may offer higher pay for certified specialists.

7. Launch an internet business
Start an online store and sell goods with various online tools. As a graphic designer, you have two options: sell your artwork digitally or print it and ship it to customers.

If you drop-ship your products, a less expensive supplier could be your partner of choice. This implies that you give your orders to a partner, who will fill them on your behalf in exchange for a cut of your sales. Using drop shipping, you can sell goods online without keeping any inventory. Instead, you buy goods from a supplier who delivers them to your clients. Because drop shipping frequently requires very little upfront investment and can be done from any location with an internet connection, it can be a great way to supplement your income or increase your primary source of income.

8. Take a ride for a delivery or ridesharing service.
You could apply to work as a ridesharing or delivery service driver, which allows users to earn money from their cars if they have a vehicle and a clean driving record. It's a flexible side gig because ridesharing and delivery services usually let you use your vehicle and set your hours. Remember that professional driving comes with additional expenses such as gas and auto insurance.

9. Trade in your gently used goods
Going through your stuff and selling the items you no longer need is another way to earn extra cash. You could offer your item to friends and family, hold a sale, or go to a consignment store in person to sell it. As an alternative, you could list your gently used items on a variety of websites and apps. If you sell online, ensure each listing has a thorough description and excellent photos. In your free time, you can also visit thrift stores to locate gently used designer goods, which you can then list for a profit.

10. Conduct a course
If you are an expert in a particular area, think about instructing beginners in a workshop, online course, or class. You could record several lectures on video and sell them on the Internet. You might also offer to give one-on-one lessons to people to teach them a skill. If you have credentials or experience in your field, this could be extremely helpful as it could increase your credibility with prospective students.

Chapter 2

The entire process of budgeting

Creating a budget is necessary to manage your finances.
A budget schedules and monitors earnings and outlays for a given time frame. Governments and businesses use budgets to track income and expenses, but you may be most familiar with them as a tool for personal financial management.

There are several kinds of budgeting techniques and systems.

How to Establish a Budget

Establishing a budget is relatively easy. The general steps involved in creating a budget are as follows: Firstly, you should determine your income and then create a spending plan.

1. Total Monthly Income

Consider all your potential revenue streams, including your job's salary, payments from clients if you work as a freelancer or gig worker, and sales from your own company. Include regular payments for child support, alimony, disability, or Social Security.

List all of your sources of income along with the average monthly amount you receive. Use the

amount you took home, not you made before taxes.
Try using a moderate amount if the amount you
receive varies monthly.

2.   Total Your Monthly Expenses
Next, compile a list of every expense you incur
every month. Add in fixed costs like your rent,
mortgage, and insurance. Next, list the costs that
vary from month to month, known as your variable
expenses. Examples include gas, entertainment, and
food (grocery and restaurant purchases).
Make an effort to keep track of all your purchases.
Pen and paper work just as well as apps and
budgeting software. You can help yourself
remember any expenses you may need to remember
by reviewing your credit card and bank statements.

3.   Take Out Expenses To Reduce Income
Lastly, deduct all of your monthly spending from
your total monthly income. If, after making this
calculation, you anticipate having money left over,
you're ahead of the game.
If you believe you won't make it, review your
spending and find any areas where you can cut or

eliminate spending. At this point, it's essential to compare needs and wants.

How to Adhere to Your Budget

Establishing a budget and adhering to it are two different things. Following a budget might necessitate doing the following:

- Keep regular track of your expenses.
- Pay with cash if you're tempted to use your debit or credit card excessively.
- Complete weekly budget check-ins to ensure you are on track for your financial goals.
- Check your budget once a month to see if there have been any changes in your income or expenses.
- Reward yourself with something small if you manage to stay within your monthly budget.
- If you have trouble adhering to your spending plan, consider finding an accountability partner who can provide support, guidance, and inspiration.

Different Budget Types

A budget compares and plans for income and expenses over a period. Creating a budget necessitates deducting expenses from income. You have an excess if you still have money. You have a deficit if your costs are higher than your income. There is a balance in the budget when revenue and expenses are equal.

Personal budgeting is more straightforward than corporate or government budgeting and involves tracking fewer expenses. Regular people create personal budgets to manage their income and expenses. Different budget strategies might be more effective for various individuals.

- Budgeting from Zero

When you use a zero-based budget, every dollar of your income is allocated. The objective is to assign a job to every dollar to ensure that money is recovered and paid. Companies, governments, and other groups can also apply this technique to budgeting.

- Budgeting with Cash Envelopes

With cash envelope budgeting, each envelope is given a specific budget category. We put the amount allocated to each budget category in an envelope.

You cannot spend any more money in that budget category for the month once you have used up all of the money in an envelope.

- Budgeting Based on Percentages

With percentage-based budgeting, funds are allocated to various categories. As an illustration, you may set aside 50% of your income for necessaries, 30% for wants, and 20% for debt repayment and savings.

Additionally, budgets can be flexible, and you are always free to create your own "rules" for budgeting. For instance, you can donate between 3% and 10% of your net income to charity.

Pros and Cons of Budgeting

Advantages:

- Offers discretion over expenditure and savings: You determine which budget categories to include and how much to allocate to each one. Additionally, you might form a regular savings habit if you pledge to save for a designated savings account, like "Hawaii Vacation."

- Aids in keeping track of spending: If you are prone to overspending, a budget allows you to track your spending, identify potentially harmful habits, and reduce unnecessary spending.
- Can lessen the strain of money: By providing a tool for preparation and emergency savings—a further layer of comfort in the event of unforeseen expenses—a budget can help lower stress levels.

Cons

- Feels restrictive: The idea that you are somehow limiting yourself is one of many people's biggest budgeting problems. To combat that, ensure your budget has space for "fun money" so you never feel shortchanged.
- Needs dedication: Budgets can assist you in taking charge of your money, but only if you follow through on your plan. You might only benefit from budgeting if you're dedicated to sticking to it.
- Depending on your ability to control your impulses: If you're used to spending money whenever you want, you might need to

develop new routines like making sure you have enough money before heading out with friends or buying a new outfit.

Reasons you should have a Budget

Having a budget is necessary to manage your finances. If you don't have a budget and constantly use credit cards or loans to make up the difference, it's easy to overspend and get into debt.

Try a few different budgeting techniques to see which suits you best. Remember that you cannot "set it and forget it" with a budget. Review your budget often and make any necessary adjustments if your income or expenses change.

Why should you create a budget?

It is impossible to overstate the significance of budgeting in terms of finances. Adhering to a budget can assist you in establishing fundamental financial practices when you are just starting.

Here are five compelling arguments for making and adhering to a budget for everyone.

1. Assists in Pursuing Long-Term Objectives
Using a budget enables you to identify and work
toward your long-term objectives. How will you
ever accumulate enough money to buy a car or make
a down payment on a house if all you do is throw
money at every shiny new thing that catches your
eye as you go through life?
A budget makes you to set objectives, save money,
monitor expenditures, and realize your aspirations.
You can map where you need to go to reach your
goal, which could be buying a house in a few years,
by observing how much money you make and spend
through a budget.

2. Can Prevent You from Going Overboard
As far too many consumers do, we owe credit cards
for all the money we spend. By the end of 2022, the
average household's credit card debt had increased
to $5,805, according to credit bureau TransUnion.
Before the invention of plastic, most people were
aware of their financial situation. They were on
track if they had enough cash left over to cover their
expenses and put some money away in savings at
the end of the month. Those who misuse and
overuse credit cards these days sometimes only

realize they're overspending once they're deeply in debt.

You're more likely to avoid this situation if you make and follow a budget. You'll be fully aware of your income, monthly spending limit, and the amount you need to save.

3. May Facilitate Retirement Savings

Assume you manage your finances sensibly, stick to your spending plan, and never carry over credit card debt past the monthly due dates. Budgeting not only helps you spend wisely but also makes saving more feasible.

Regular savings and investment contributions should be a part of your budget. You will eventually accumulate a sizable nest egg when you set aside a portion of your monthly earnings to contribute to your 401(k), individual retirement account (IRA), or other retirement funds. The short-term sacrifices might be necessary, but they will pay off in the long run.

4. Can Show Spending Patterns

Creating a budget compels you to examine your spending patterns. When looking over your spending, you might discover that you're paying for unnecessary items like a cable TV subscription. Using a budget, you can reconsider your spending patterns and refocus your financial objectives.

If you look at your monthly spending, you might discover that you spent more money on eating out than home cooking for one month. As a result, you can review your budget and make necessary adjustments. You might decide to reduce the amount you devote to luxury or unnecessary spending in place of saving money for a new car or a significant home improvement project that could also increase the value of your property if you find that you are going over the target amounts you set in your budget for such discretionary items.

Chapter 3

Gaining knowledge about future savings

Savings: What Are They?
The amount of money left over after deducting
consumer expenditure from disposable income over
a specified period is called savings. Therefore,
savings is a person's or household's net financial
surplus after all bills and commitments have been
settled.
Cash and its equivalents, such as bank deposits and
store savings. These assets have no risk of loss but
also provide very little return. However, investing
requires putting money at risk to increase savings.
The money that's left over after expenses is saved.
Individuals may set aside money for various
objectives in life, including retirement, a child's
college education, a down payment on a house or
vehicle, a trip, and several other things.
One can be said to be living paycheck to paycheck if
they cannot save money. In an emergency, such a
person typically does not have enough cash to get
by, and they run the risk of incurring debt or
declaring bankruptcy.

Savings Account Types

Banks offer various savings account types, each with unique features and restrictions. The Federal Deposit Insurance Corporation (FDIC) insures up to $250,000 in bank savings accounts for each depositor.

1. Savings Account

Interest is paid on funds in a savings account set aside for emergencies but not for regular spending. You can make deposits and withdrawals via phone, mail, internet, in-person bank branches, and ATMs. Savings account interest rates are more than those on checking accounts but are still generally low. Online savings accounts usually offer better rates of return due to their higher interest payments. High-yield savings accounts, which can provide up to 20–25 times higher interest on deposits than the national average, may include accounts only available online.

2. Checking Accounts

To write checks and use debit cards that deduct money from your account are features of a checking account. Compared to other bank accounts, checking accounts have lower interest rates, and many don't

charge checking customers any interest.
Nonetheless, account holders receive highly liquid
and easily accessible funds in exchange, frequently
with minimal or no monthly fees.

3. Money Market Accounts

Not to be confused with a money market fund, a
money market account (MMA) is an interest-bearing
account at a bank or credit union. Regular passbook
savings accounts typically offer lower interest rates,
while money market accounts (MMAs) offer
additional benefits like debit card and check writing
capabilities. These are less flexible than a standard
checking account because of the applicable
limitations.

Beginning to save money can be the most
challenging task of all. You can keep all your short-
and long-term goals by following this step-by-step
guide to help you create a realistic approach.

1. Keep a record of your spending.

Determining your spending is the first step towards
starting a savings plan. Record every penny you
spend, including regular monthly bills and the cost

of every coffee, household item, and gratuity.
Whatever method works best for you is how you
keep track of your spending: pen and paper, a basic
spreadsheet, or a free online app or spending tracker.
After you have your data, total each amount and
arrange the numbers into categories like groceries,
gas, and mortgage. Verify that everything is
included by consulting your bank and credit card
statements.

2. Make savings a part of your budget.
Now that you know your monthly expenses, start
making a budget. To help you plan your spending
and prevent overspending, your budget should
display how your expenses compare to your income.
Remember to account for costs like auto
maintenance that happen frequently but not every
month. Ensure your budget has a savings category,
and start saving as much as you feel comfortable
with. Eventually, it would help if you aimed to
increase your savings by as much as 15–20 percent
of your income.

3. Look for methods to reduce your spending.
It might be time to make spending reductions if you
cannot save as much as you want. Find non-

essentials you can cut back on, like entertainment
and eating out. Seek methods to reduce the cost of
your monthly expenses, such as your phone plan or
auto insurance. Other suggestions for reducing
regular costs are as follows:

4. Look for things to do for free.
Use resources to locate free or inexpensive
entertainment, such as listings for local events.

- Examine recurring expenses
- Get rid of any memberships and subscriptions
  you don't use, especially if they renew
  automatically.
- Compare the cost of cooking at home versus
  eating out.
- Make it a point to eat most of your meals at
  home, and on the nights you want to treat
  yourself, look into deals at nearby
  restaurants.
- Hold off on purchasing.
- When tempted to buy something
  unnecessary, hold off for a few days. You
  might find that the item was more of a desire
  than a necessity, in which case you could
  create a plan to save money.

5. Establish savings objectives.
Establishing a goal is among the best strategies to save money. Consider your potential savings goals first, both short-term (one to three years) and long-term (four or more years). Next, project the amount of money you'll require and the potential time it will take you to save it.

6. Establish your priorities when it comes to
     money.
Your goals will influence how you share your savings after your income and expenses. For instance, you could set money aside for a new car if you anticipate needing one shortly. But remember long-term objectives; retirement planning should be addressed in favor of pressing matters. You can clearly understand how to distribute your savings by learning how to rank your savings objectives.

7. Select the appropriate equipment.
Numerous investment and savings accounts are appropriate for short- and long-term objectives. And you're not limited to choosing just one. Scrutinize all your options, considering fees, interest rates, balance minimums, risk, and when you need the money.

This will help you determine the best combination to save for your objectives.

- Short-term objectives

Consider using one of these FDIC-insured deposit accounts if you need to be able to access the money quickly or if you need to need it soon.

- An account for savings

A certificate of deposit (CD), usually offers a higher interest rate than a savings account, allows you to lock in your money for a predetermined time.
Long-term objectives
When putting money down for your child's education or retirement, take into account:

Securities like stocks or mutual funds, FDIC-insured individual retirement accounts (IRAs), or 529 plans are tax-efficient savings accounts. These investment products are accessible through investment accounts with a broker-dealer.

8. Set up automatic savings.
Automated transfers between your savings and checking accounts are available at almost all banks.

You can decide where, when, and how much money to transfer. You can even split your direct deposit, which allows you to set aside a certain amount of each paycheck for savings. The benefit is that you won't have to consider it and are less inclined to spend the money elsewhere. Credit card rewards and spare change programs, which round up transactions to dollar and deposit the difference into a savings or investment account, are two more simple ways to save money.

9. Observe your savings increase.
Every month, evaluate your spending plan and track your advancement. This will assist you in staying accurate to your personal savings plan and promptly recognize and resolve issues. Knowing how to save money motivates you to develop new ideas to reach your objectives more quickly.

Chapter 4

Investing: making long-lasting investments.

What does investing entail?

Investing, in general, is the process of using money to work for a while on a project or endeavor to make positive returns (i.e., profits that exceed the amount of the initial investment). It distributes resources, most commonly capital or money, to make a profit or achieve other objectives.

Investing can take many forms (directly or indirectly). For example, one can use capital to launch a business or buy assets like real estate to rent them out and sell them at a profit in the future. Investing is not the same as saving because the money used is put to work, implying an implicit risk that the associated project or projects could fail and result in a financial loss. Speculation differs from investing because the latter involves betting on short-term price fluctuations rather than putting the money to work.

Knowing How to Invest

Investing allows money to increase in value over time. The fundamental tenet of investing is the expecting of a positive return in the form of income or statistically significant price appreciation. There is a vast array of assets in which one can invest and reap financial rewards.

In investing, risk and return go hand in hand; lower risk typically translates into lower expected returns, while higher returns are usually associated with higher risk. Essential investments like Certificates of Deposit (CDs) are at the low-risk end of the risk spectrum; equities and stocks are considered riskier, while bonds and other fixed-income instruments are higher up the risk scale. Derivatives and commodities are typically regarded as some of the most challenging investment options. Moreover, one can put money into fragile things like fine art and antiques or valuable things like land or real estate. Expectations for risk and return can differ significantly, even within the same asset class. A micro-cap that trades on a smaller exchange will have a different risk-return profile than a blue-chip that trades on the New York Stock Exchange.

The kind of asset determines the returns it produces. Bonds typically pay interest every quarter, but many stocks pay dividends every quarter. Different forms of income are subject to varying tax rates in numerous jurisdictions.

Investment Types

These days, most investments are connected to financial instruments that let people or companies raise and use capital for businesses. These businesses then rake that capital toward expansion or revenue-producing ventures.

Although there are many different kinds of investments, the following are the most popular ones:

1. Stocks

Purchasing stock entitles a buyer to a portion of the company's ownership. A company's shareholders are those who own its stock and have the opportunity to benefit from growth and success through regular dividend payments deducted from the company's profits as well as price appreciation of the stock.

2. Bonds:

Bonds are the debt obligations of corporations, governments, and municipalities. Purchasing a bond indicates that you are taking on a portion of the debt of the issuing company and that you will be paid interest on the bond regularly and get your money back when it matures.

3. Funds

Investment managers oversee funds, pooled instruments that let investors buy stocks, bonds, preferred shares, commodities, and other securities. Mutual and exchange-traded funds, or ETFs, are two of the most popular funds. ETFs trade on stock exchanges and, like stocks, are valued continuously throughout the trading day; mutual funds do not trade on an exchange but are valued at the end. ETFs and mutual funds have two options: fund managers can actively manage them,

5. Trusts for Investments

Another kind of pooled investment is a trust. Real Estate Investment Trusts (REITs) are among the most well-liked in this category within this category.

Real estate investment trusts (REITs) regularly allocate a portion of their rental income from residential and commercial properties to their investors. Because REITs are listed on stock exchanges, their investors can benefit from immediate liquidity.

6. Investments Alternatives
Private equity and hedge funds are included in the broad category of alternative investments. Hedge funds get their name because they can use long and short positions in stocks and other assets to diversify their investment bets. Companies can raise money without going public, thanks to private equity. Historically, wealthy individuals who satisfied specific income and net worth criteria and were referred to as "accredited investors" were the only ones with access to hedge funds and private equity. On the other hand, retail investors can now access alternative investments thanks to the introduction of fund formats in recent years.

7. Alternative Derivatives and Options
Financial instruments known as derivatives are valued against another financial instrument, like an index or stock. Popular derivatives like options

contracts give the buyer the option, but not the duty, to purchase or sell a security at a fixed price within a predetermined time window. Derivatives are typically risky investments with significant potential returns since they use leverage.

8. Commodities
Currency and financial instruments are examples of commodities, metals, oil, grain, and animal products. Commodity futures are contracts to buy or sell a certain amount of a commodity at a given price on a specific future date. They can be traded through ETFs or other commodity futures. It is possible to utilize commodities for speculation as well as risk-hedging.

How to Make Investments
Self-Doing Investing
Whether you are a do-it-yourself (DIY) investor or would rather have your money managed by a professional is the key to answering the "how to invest" question. Because of their cheap commissions and the simplicity of executing trades on their platforms, discount or online brokerages are

the preferred choice of many investors who would
instead manage their funds.

DIY investing, also known as self-directed
investing, calls for reasonable knowledge, expertise,
time, and emotional restraint. If any of these
qualities don't fit you, let an expert handle your
financial affairs.

Investments Handled by Professionals
Professional money managers typically look after
the investments of investors who prefer that service.
Wealth managers usually charge their clients as a
percentage of assets under management. These
investors are willing to pay a premium for the
convenience of having an expert handle their
research, trading, and investment decision-making,
even though it is more expensive than managing
their funds.

Investing With A Roboadvisor
Some investors make investigators make automated
financial advisor recommendations. Robo-advisors
use artificial intelligence and algorithms to collect
vital investor data and their risk tolerance to provide

relevant recommendations. Robo-advisors, which provide services akin to those of a human investment advisor, are affordable to invest in with little to no human intervention. Technology has advanced to the point where Robo-advisors can now do more than recommend investments. In addition, they can assist individuals with managing trusts and other retirement accounts, like 401(k)s and retirement plans.

How a novice should invest

Select a strategy for your first investments based on how much you want to invest when reaching your goals and how much risk you can tolerate.
When you start, rent, utilities, debt payments, and groceries seem all you can afford. This is especially true in inflationary times when your paycheck doesn't go as far toward buying a house, a car, or bread. However, it's time to start investing after you've worked out a budget for those monthly costs and put some money aside in an emergency fund. Choosing what to invest in and how much is the problematic part.

As a novice to the world of investing, you will have many questions, not the least: How much money do I need? How do I start? What are the best investment strategies for novices? These and other queries will be addressed in our guide.

To begin investing, follow these five steps:

1. Invest as soon as you can
Investing when you're young is one of the best ways to see good returns on your money. Compound earnings are responsible for this, as your investment returns begin to generate their returns. With compounding, the balance in your account can increase over time.

In addition, many people ponder whether they can start with a small amount of money. To put it briefly, absolutely.
Thanks to fractional shares, low or nonexistent investment minimums, and zero commissions, investing with smaller sums of money is now more feasible than ever. Many investment options, including mutual funds, exchange-traded funds, and

index funds, are accessible for comparatively small sums of money.

2. Choose the amount to put in.
Your financial situation, your investing goal, and the deadline for achieving it will all determine how much you should invest.
Retirement is one popular investment objective. Generally speaking, you should save between 10% and 15% of your annual income for retirement. Although it may seem unachievable, you can gradually increase it by starting small. (Use our retirement calculator to determine a more precise retirement goal.)

Your first investing milestone is simple if your employer offers matching contributions for retirement accounts like 401(k)s: Contribute at least enough to the account to receive the entire match. You should take advantage of that free money since your employer match contributes to that total.
For other investment objectives, like buying a house, going on a trip, or funding your schooling, figure out how much you need to invest each month or every week based on your time horizon.

3. Create an account for investments.
Suppose you're among the many people saving for retirement but need access to a 401(k) or other employer-sponsored retirement account. In that case, you can save for retirement using an individual retirement account (IRA), such as a Roth or traditional IRA.

Retirement accounts, intended for retirement and have limitations on when and how you can withdraw your money, are something you should stay away from if you're investing for another purpose. Consider a taxable brokerage account instead, which allows you to withdraw money at any time without incurring additional fees or taxes. Suppose an individual has reached their maximum IRA retirement contribution and wants to invest. Brokerage accounts are a good choice because IRA contribution limits are typically much lower than employer-sponsored retirement accounts.

4. Decide on an investment plan.

Your time horizon determines your investment plan, savings objectives, and the money you need to achieve them.

You can put almost all your money in stocks if your savings goal, such as retirement, is over 20 years away. To invest in stocks, most people find that low-cost stock mutual funds, index funds, or exchange-traded funds (ETFs) are the best options because selecting individual stocks can be difficult and time-consuming.

Since stocks carry risk, you would be better off keeping your money in an online savings account, or low-risk investment if you are saving for a short-term goal and need it within five years. The top choices for immediate savings are outlined here.

If you cannot decide, you can open an investment account, including an IRA, with a robo-advisor. A robo-advisor is an investment management service that creates and manages your investment portfolio using computer algorithms.

Low-cost index funds and ETFs comprise most of the portfolios constructed by robo-advisors. Robots allow you to get started quickly because they offer low costs and low or no minimum requirements.

They charge a nominal fee for portfolio management, typically equal to 0.25% of your account balance.

5. Recognize the options you have for investments. You must select what to invest in after determining how to invest. Risk is associated with every investment, so it's critical to comprehend each one, its level of risk, and whether or not it fits with your objectives.

Conclusion

Although most people aspire to be wealthy, only some know how to get there. Despite what the general public believes, you don't need much money to start down the path to riches—many of the wealthiest people in the world had very modest beginnings. What is their secret, then?

The response is straightforward: it all comes down to money management. Compared to most people, business owners have more control over their income. This implies that you can accumulate a significant amount of wealth if you're wise about it. But it's about more than generating as much money as possible; you also need to know how to invest and save your money sensibly.

Among the wealthy's secrets are

Investing in oneself first is one of the wealthiest people's best-kept secrets. They constantly search for methods to expand their knowledge and skill set because they recognize their success is based on their hard work and abilities.

As entrepreneurs, this is what you ought to be doing as well. Make constant investments in your learning and growth to advance in your field. You will earn more money if you are more valuable. Furthermore,

accumulating wealth will be simpler the more
money you make.

Living below their means is another secret of the
rich. Regardless of their income, they consistently
seek ways to maximize their savings and
investments. They realize that what matters is how
much money you keep, not how much you make.
One more thing about the rich: they usually have
more than one source of income. They will then
have other streams to turn to if one dries up. You are
in a great position to generate multiple sources of
income for yourself as a business owner.
For instance, you may launch a business-related
blog or podcast and charge for sponsorships or
advertising. Alternatively, you may design an online
course and impart your knowledge to others. The
options are virtually limitless, but the key is to
diversify your sources of income to avoid ever
having all of your eggs in one basket.